THE STORY OF A
JUMBO JET

Kingfisher Books, Grisewood & Dempsey Ltd,
Elsley House, 24–30 Great Titchfield Street,
London W1P 7AD

First published in 1990 by Kingfisher Books

10 9 8 7 6

BRITISH LIBRARY CATALOGUING IN PUBLICATION DATA
Royston, Angela
    Jumbo jet.
    1. Commercial passenger aeroplanes
    I. Title   II. Buchanan, George   III. Series
    629.133340423
ISBN 0 86272 538 0

With thanks to Air Commodore Yetman of the British Airline
Pilot Association, and to British Airways

Edited by Veronica Pennycook
Designed by Ben White
Cover design by Terry Woodley
Phototypeset by Southern Positives and Negatives (SPAN),
Lingfield, Surrey
Printed in Spain

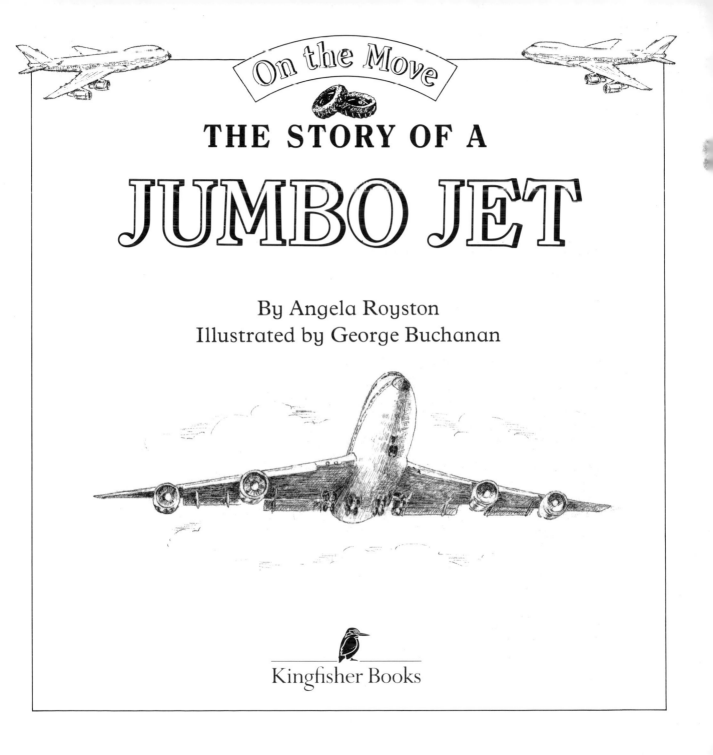

On the Move

THE STORY OF A

JUMBO JET

By Angela Royston

Illustrated by George Buchanan

Kingfisher Books

The plane in this story is a Boeing 747. It can carry over 400 passengers and is the biggest passenger aircraft.

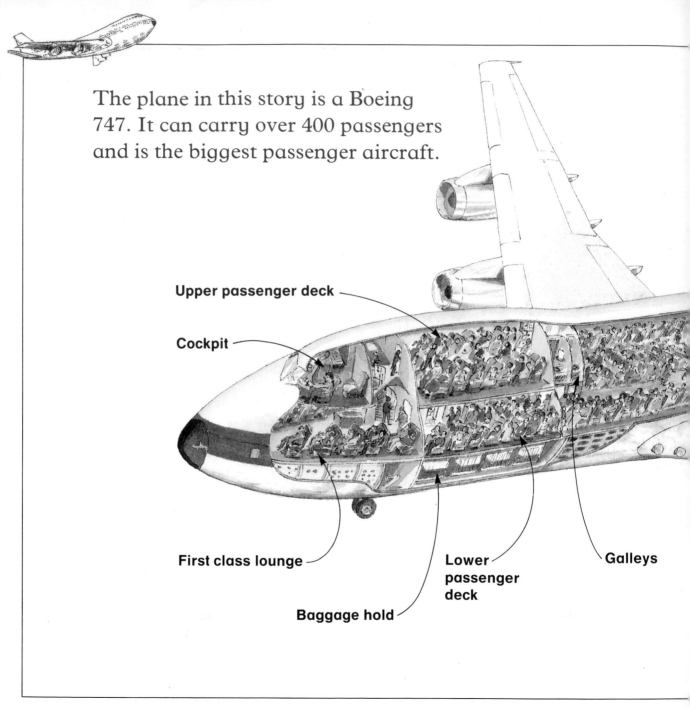

Upper passenger deck

Cockpit

First class lounge

Baggage hold

Lower passenger deck

Galleys

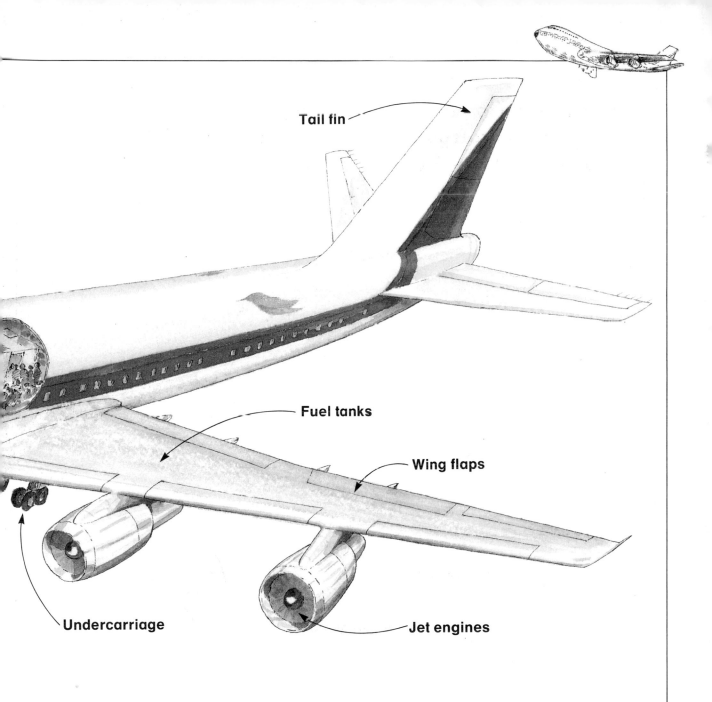

Tail fin

Fuel tanks

Wing flaps

Undercarriage

Jet engines

The jumbo jet taxis out to the runway at an airport in New York. It is morning and many planes are taking off and landing. Tom, the pilot of the jumbo jet, hears a message from the control tower on his earphones: "Bluebird 202 cleared for take-off."

So Tom pushes the throttle forward. The jet engines roar as they build up power and the jumbo jet starts to speed down the runway. Kate, the co-pilot, calls out the plane's speed to Tom, "100 knots, 120, 130... take-off!"

Tom pulls the control column and the heavy plane rises smoothly into the air. He moves another lever to pull up the undercarriage and then the plane climbs high above the ground. Some of the passengers look out of the jumbo jet's windows.

They have left the airport far below. Even New York's skyscrapers now look like matchboxes. The plane climbs higher still, up through the clouds and into the sunshine above them. The jumbo jet is on its way to London.

Air Traffic Control tells Kate how high to fly and
which route to take and she taps this into the plane's
computer. Now Tom switches over to automatic
pilot so that the plane will fly itself. Tom, Kate and
John, the engineer, watch the dials to make sure
that everything is working properly.

Then Kate sees a black blob on the weather radar.
"Thunderstorm ahead," she says. Tom taps a new
route into the computer so that the jumbo jet will
avoid the storm.

Meanwhile, the passengers are settling down in their seats ready for the long journey ahead. It will take the jumbo jet nearly seven hours to fly to London. Maria and the rest of the cabin crew heat up a meal in the plane's ovens for everyone.

Maria loads up her trolley with food and takes it along to the passengers. "Just look at those black clouds," one boy says to Maria. "Yes," she replies, "there's a big thunderstorm going on over there, but we're going around it."

The plane has been flying for five hours when John suddenly notices that one of the dials has lit up. He checks the other dials and sees that the oil pressure is low. "Engine number three is overheating," he says to Tom.

Tom takes that engine off automatic control. He
makes it work more slowly so that it quickly cools
down. "I'll report it to ground crew when we land,"
he says. The jumbo jet flies smoothly on and the sun
begins to set. They will soon reach London airport.

When the plane begins to fly down, Maria checks
that all the passengers have fastened their seat
belts. Radio instruments guide Tom to the runway
and show him how high the plane should be. The
jumbo jet gets lower and lower and soon Tom can
see the lights on the runway ahead.

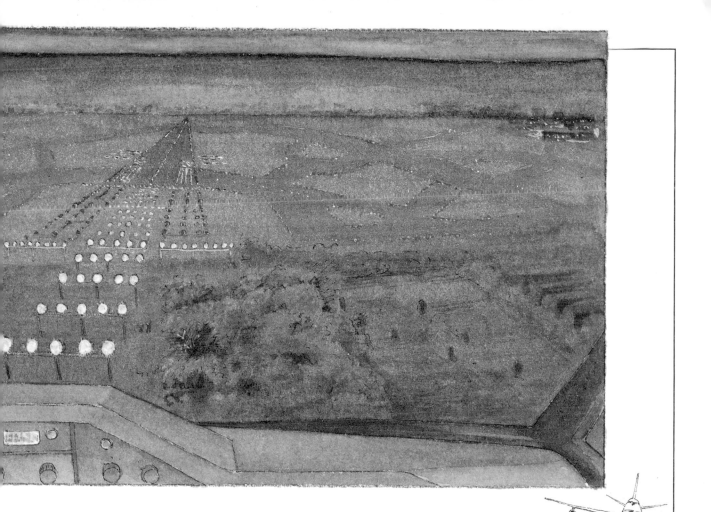

Tom lowers the flaps on the wings to help the plane slow down. "Bluebird 202 cleared to land," radios the control tower and Tom lowers the wheels. The plane skims over a bar of green lights and a few seconds later the wheels touch the ground. Quickly, Tom uses the brakes and engines to stop the plane.

The jumbo jet taxis towards the passenger buildings and Tom stops the engines.

Jetties are joined to the doors of the plane so the passengers walk straight into the airport buildings.

Baggage trolleys unload the suitcases and cleaners arrive to clean the inside of the plane.

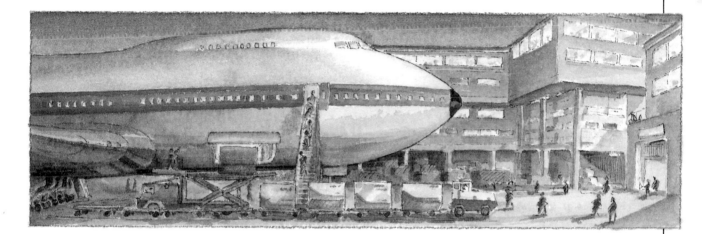

A petrol tanker refills the plane's tanks with fuel from an underground tank.

Tom tells Lee, the ground engineer, about the problem with engine number three. "I'll have a look at it right away," says Lee. Tom then joins the air crew who are going off to rest.

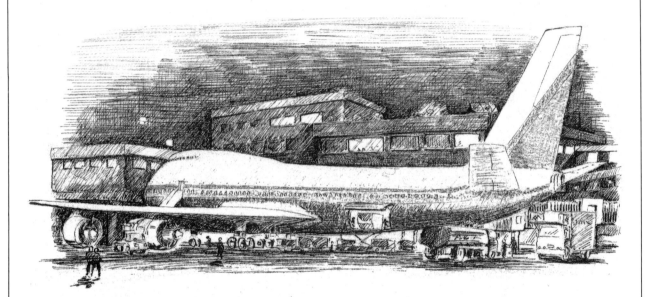

Lee and another engineer are lifted up to the engine. They take off part of the cowling and look inside using special instruments. "We'll have to change this engine," says Lee.

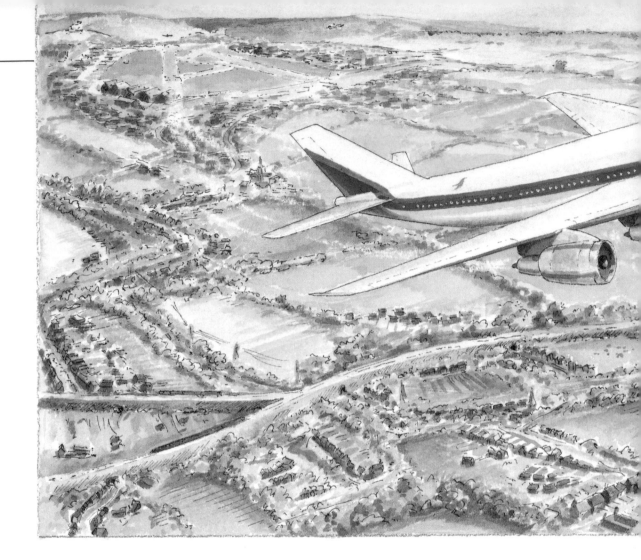

It is just getting light when the jumbo jet is ready to fly again. The passengers and luggage come on board while the new crew check that everything is working smoothly. Then Ian, the new pilot, tells the steward to close and lock the doors.

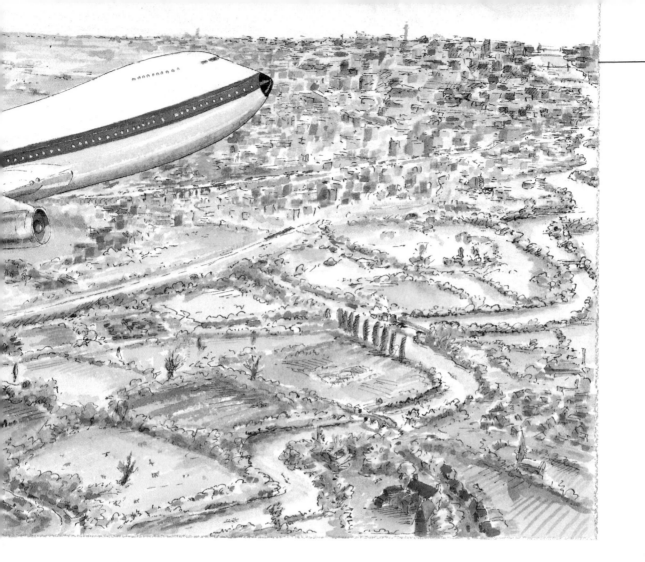

The jetty is taken away and Ian starts the engines.
At the end of the runway Ian lowers the wing flaps
so they will help the plane to lift up into the air. The
message comes over the radio that they are cleared
for take-off. Next stop Jamaica!

Some Special Words

Air Traffic Control A group of people who control where and when aircraft can fly.

Automatic pilot An instrument which keeps a plane flying to a set height, direction and speed.

Control column A lever which makes a plane fly higher or lower.

Control tower A building at an airport with computers, radar and people working in Air Traffic Control.

Cowling The outer covering of a plane's engine.

Flaps Parts of the wings which can be moved to help control the plane's speed.

Jetty A large passageway which passengers walk through to get on and off the plane.

Oil pressure This shows if the oil is flowing round the engine to keep it working well.

Radar An instrument which detects large objects and shows them on a screen.

Steward/Stewardess The people who look after the passengers during a flight.

Taxis A plane taxis when it moves on its wheels along the ground.

Throttle A lever which increases or decreases the power of the engines.